SIGHTSEERS
ESSENTIAL TRAVEL GUIDES TO THE PAST

CALIFORNIA

GOLD RUSH

A GUIDE TO CALIFORNIA
IN THE 1850s

JULIE FERRIS

KINGFISHER

NEW YORK

Written and edited by Julie Ferris
Senior Designer Jane Tassie

Consultant Christina Parker
Illustrations Inklink Firenze
Kevin Maddison
Ray Grinaway

KINGFISHER
Larousse Kingfisher Chambers Inc.
95 Madison Avenue
New York, New York 10016

First published in 1999
2 4 6 8 10 9 7 5 3 1

1TR(IDDS/IEB)/0399/WKT/UNV(UNV)/140MA

LIBRARY OF CONGRESS CATALOGING-IN-PUBLICATION DATA
Ferris, Julie.
California Gold Rush/by Julie Ferris.
p. cm.—(Sightseers)
Includes index.
Summary: Presents a looks at the sites and society that existed in
San Francisco during the time of the Gold Rush in the 1850s.
1. San Francisco Bay Area (Calif.)—Social life and customs—19th
century—Juvenile literature. 2. Frontier and pioneer life—California—San
Francisco Bay Area—Juvenile literature. 3. California—Gold discoveries—Juvenile
literature. 4. San Francisco Bay Area (Calif.)—Guidebooks—Juvenile literature.
[1. San Francisco Bay Area (Calif.)—Social life and customs—19th
century. 2. Frontier and pioneer life—California—San Francisco
Bay Area. 3. California—Gold discoveries.] I. Title. II. Series.
F869.S35F47 1999
979.4'6—dc21 98–50415 CIP AC

ISBN 0-7534-5218-9

Printed in Hong Kong

Contents

Introducing California

California was a Mexican province until 1848, when it was claimed by United States troops. In 1850, it became the 31st state.

Until the discovery of gold in 1848, California was little more than a collection of Franciscan missions, cattle ranches, and thinly populated coastal towns. As news of the gold find spread, people from all over the world began flocking to the area to seek their fortunes.

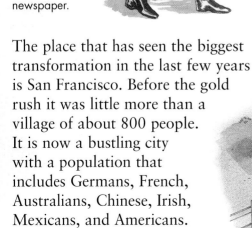

Because of the vast numbers of prospectors who traveled to California in 1849, gold seekers are often nicknamed "forty-niners." You may be able to pick up a souvenir cartoon of a miner in a magazine or newspaper.

The place that has seen the biggest transformation in the last few years is San Francisco. Before the gold rush it was little more than a village of about 800 people. It is now a bustling city with a population that includes Germans, French, Australians, Chinese, Irish, Mexicans, and Americans.

4

San Francisco has a warm climate, but fog is common in the summer months.

You may encounter language problems because of the many nationalities.

Watch out! The streets of San Francisco are not paved—let alone paved with gold!

Gold can be found as flakes, dust, or nuggets. Mining is hard work and few make their fortunes here.

San Francisco is an exciting place to visit. The harbor is packed with ships, and every day 30 new buildings are built. Theaters, hotels, and saloons have sprung up all over the city.

Sightseers' tip

Many of the ships in the harbor have been abandoned by passengers and crews rushing off to the gold diggings.

Getting there

Merchants' Express Line of Clipper Ships
FOR
SAN FRANCISCO!
NONE BUT A 1 FAST SAILING CLIPPERS LOADED IN THIS LINE.

THE EXTREME CLIPPER SHIP
OCEAN EXPRESS
WATSON, COMMANDER,
AT PIER 9, EAST RIVER.

This splendid vessel is one of the fastest Clippers afloat, and a great favorite with all shippers. Her commander, Capt. WATSON, was formerly master of the celebrated Clipper "FLYING DRAGON," which made the passage in 97 days, and of the ship "POLYNESIA," which made the passage in 103 days.

She comes to the berth one third loaded, and has very large engagements.

RANDOLPH M. COOLEY,
118 WATER ST., cor. Wall, Tontine Building.
Agents in San Francisco, DE WITT, KITTLE & Co.

The best way to get to San Francisco is by sea. You can either travel around South America's Cape Horn, or via Panama. The Cape Horn journey can take seven months, and you will have to contend with storms, overcrowding, and boredom. The Panama route is quicker, but more expensive. Travelers have to pay extra to cross the narrow neck of land between North and South America.

Sea travelers are often called "argonauts," named after adventurers in Greek mythology who sailed with the hero Jason on his ship the *Argo* in search of the Golden Fleece.

San Francisco has no docks, so you have to wade through mud to reach the shore.

 A sea voyage is the only option if traveling in the winter.

 Ships are often so crowded that you may have to sleep in a lifeboat.

Sightseers' tip Overland travelers will need a very well-equipped wagon. Remember you will be crossing plains, deserts, rivers, and mountains, and covering only about 20 miles a day.

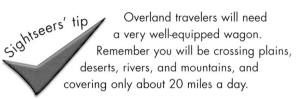

If you are planning to pan for gold during your stay in San Francisco, a strong mule will help you carry your mining equipment.

Those who choose to travel overland can join other travelers on the banks of the Missouri River. Make sure you pack plenty of food, tools, and bedding in your wagon. Although the wagons are uncomfortable (they have no springs), they are sturdy and practical. Most people use oxen to haul their wagons. They are strong, can travel farther than horses without water, and can be eaten if you run out of food.

What to wear

Practical clothing is a must for visitors to California. Wool shirts and heavy pants are commonly worn by miners and are ideal for the rough, outdoor life they lead. Make sure you bring a pair of sturdy boots with you. They will protect your feet from the ankle-deep mud that floods the streets of San Francisco.

For the ultimate gold rush souvenir why not buy a woolen shirt with a pick-and-shovel motif?

Sightseers' tip

Make sure you wear a wide-brimmed hat to protect you from the sun while panning for gold. Try rubbing bear fat into the leather of your boots to make them waterproof.

8

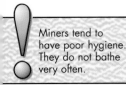
Miners tend to have poor hygiene. They do not bathe very often.

You will be on your feet all day, so make sure you bring a sturdy pair of shoes.

As with everything else in California, clothes are very expensive.

Thousands of Chinese immigrants have flocked to California in recent years. Many dress in the traditional Chinese style, wearing pointed, broad-brimmed hats and loose-fitting clothes. The men grow their hair long and tie it in a single braid.

Many Chinese immigrants have opened up laundries in the mining camps and towns. For a small price, they will take in your dirty clothes and wash them for you.

Long skirts, petticoats, and bonnets are standard wear for women and girls. Some women dress in men's clothes so they can work more freely and avoid unwanted attention from men.

Don't worry about getting a haircut, as uncut, unwashed, and uncombed hair is highly fashionable. Long, unkempt beards and whiskers are also de rigueur. This is just as well—most of the region's barbers have gone prospecting in the gold mines. Although many residents of California do not concern themselves with good hygiene and cleanliness, there are plenty of bathhouses in San Francisco. You can make your own soap by boiling water, wood ash, and bear fat together in a big kettle.

Food and drink

The wide variety of restaurants in San Francisco offers the discerning traveler the chance to sample many traditional foods from all over the world. American, French, German, Mexican, and Chinese cooking styles can all be found in this cosmopolitan city.

It has become a custom to celebrate a lucky strike in the gold mines with a feast of oysters.

Despite the large selection of food available, most miners have a very poor diet. Food is expensive, particularly outside San Francisco. Fresh vegetables, fruit, and dairy products are very hard to find— farming in the region has largely been abandoned as farm workers have flocked to the gold mines.

A pound of potatoes costs 1¢ in New York, but costs $1 in California.

Meats available include beef, mutton, grizzly bear, deer, and turtle.

Many miners use their gold pans as food plates when camping.

Food is usually cooked over an open fire in the camps. Meals are a time to relax and socialize.

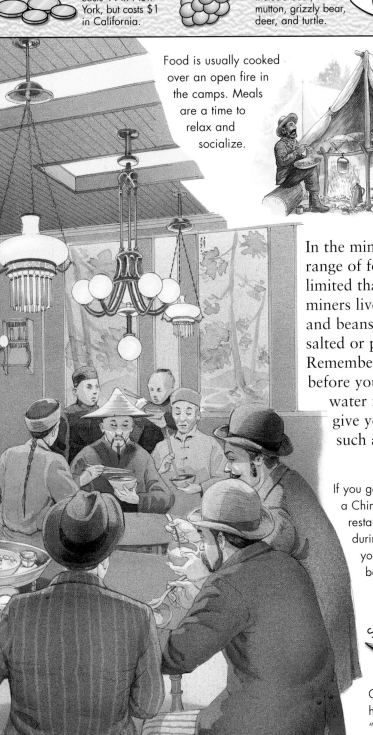

In the mining camps, the range of food available is more limited than in the city. Most miners live on a diet of pork and beans. The pork is usually salted or pickled to preserve it. Remember to boil any water before you drink it. River water is not clean and may give you a serious infection such as dysentery.

If you go to a Chinese restaurant during your stay in San Francisco you will have to eat from a bowl with chopsticks.

Sightseers' tip

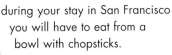
Chinese eating-houses have a very good reputation in California. Look out for flags hanging over the doors with "Enter and depart in peace" written in Chinese characters.

11

Shopping

Although pricey, San Francisco is a great place to shop. You will be able to buy everything from food, clothes, household goods, and mining tools to luxury items that include Chinese shawls and fans. You can even buy exotic pets such as brightly colored parrots and raccoons.

A daguerreotype (photograph) framed in Californian gold makes a great souvenir of your trip.

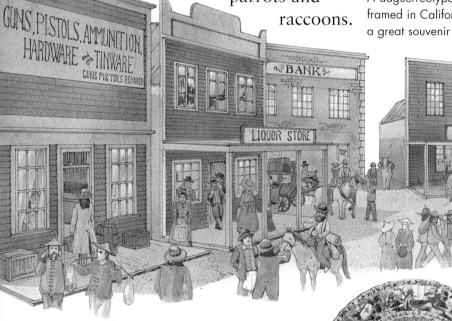

Make sure to visit Chinatown. The stores are packed with luxury goods such as this beautiful fan.

If you are planning a trip to the gold mines, you will need to purchase mining and camping equipment. The storekeeper should be able to help you choose the tools you will need.

Camp stores sometimes offer overnight shelter to new arrivals.

In newer mining camps, the store acts as a social center for miners.

Traveling artists (failed miners) will, for a price, sketch your diggings.

California is a *very* expensive place to shop! Most miners earn about $10 a day, but a dozen eggs can set you back $4 and a single apple can cost as much as $1. San Francisco has attracted many entrepreneurs. One ship's captain brought a shipload of stray cats to the city and sold them as rat catchers at $10 apiece.

You will find a general store at the center of most mining camps. As well as supplying miners with essential goods and tools, the store often acts as a bar and gambling den. Every store has a set of scales to weigh the gold dust used by the miners in place of money. Storekeepers will usually offer credit— unless you prove to be a bad risk!

Sightseers' tip
Abandoned ships are often run aground and leased as stores and hotels. You may well see some nestling among other buildings on the streets of San Francisco.

Accommodation

Many houses have been prefabricated in the eastern states and shipped around Cape Horn to California.

Y ou will have no problem finding accommodation to suit your budget in San Francisco. If you can't afford to stay in one of the fine hotels on Portsmouth Square, you could opt for a bed in a boardinghouse or dormitory. If your budget is really tight, why not just pitch a tent in one of the mining camps?

While some cabins are very isolated, others are grouped together, forming small towns.

Many miners have built themselves log cabins near their claim. The cabins are usually quite small and cramped. Window glass is very expensive, but some miners have made their own windows by cutting the flat ends from glass jars and gluing several of them into a frame using mud.

Make sure you have a good supply of candles to provide light in your cabin in the evenings.

Prices range from $37 a week for a hotel room to $6 a week for a dormitory bed.

 Many hotels host entertainment and gambling in the evenings.

Watch out for snakes—they go everywhere, including beds!

HOTEL

San Francisco's grandest hotel is Parker House on Portsmouth Square. The White Cheer House Hotel on Sacramento Street, however, is the only one with bathtubs.

Sightseers' tip

Boardinghouses and hotels in San Francisco don't usually have backyards. You will often see people talking and children playing on the wooden sidewalks and on the dusty streets in front of their lodgings.

Prospecting for gold

Making your fortune at the gold diggings is not very likely. However, a day spent prospecting would be an interesting excursion, and you never know, you could be lucky! All you need to do is stake your claim on a promising piece of land.

Sightseers' tip Watch out! Newcomers are usually directed to land in mines such as Poverty Bars, Coyote Diggings, Old Dry Diggings, and Rough and Ready, which have already been thoroughly worked over.

Make sure you follow the miners' strict rules for staking a claim.

Wear comfortable, hard-wearing clothes— you will be out in the elements all day.

Gold dust can be used in stores to pay for food and goods.

Gold is usually found in layers of rock. River water eats away the rock and exposes the gold, then carries it downstream. Look in bends in the river, where the water slows down and deposits the gold.

You can take any gold dust you find to a local bank. They will weigh it and pay you the going rate— about $1 for 30 grams.

The initial rush of gold fever has used up all the surface gold. So digging for gold is now tedious, backbreaking work. The simplest method of prospecting is panning. This means spending hours squatting in ice-cold water, rotating the pan to separate the gold from the earth. Most miners work in teams, using a cradle or a Long Tom to speed up the sorting. You can identify gold if you bite it or hammer it—fool's gold will flake.

You will need only simple tools for a day's prospecting— pickaxes to break up the rock, shovels to move the earth and stones, and a pan.

Visit a saloon

To get a true taste of California life, make sure you visit one of the many saloons and gambling dens. In the dimly lit, smoke-filled saloons, bartenders serve drinks, gossip is exchanged, and business deals are made. The saloons are often elaborately decorated, with ornate fixtures shipped from all over the world. Watch out for the spittoons placed on the floor for the benefit of tobacco-chewers.

There are few women in mining towns and men often have to take women's roles in dances. The man who dons a hoopskirt becomes the "belle of the ball"!

Alcohol has many nicknames, including "rotgut," "devil's brew," and "firewater."

! Watch out for professional gamblers who usually cheat to make sure they win.

Saloonkeepers tend to make more money than gold miners.

Sightseers' tip Miners often pay for drinks with gold dust. When the saloon closes, enterprising children run wet pins between the floorboards to pick up any spilled dust.

The saloons often put on musical entertainment to encourage business. Female singers are especially popular.

If you would like to try your luck at cards you will have no problem finding a game to join. There are over 1,000 gambling dens in San Francisco alone. Popular games include Faro and Twenty-One.

The gambling halls are very profitable for their owners and many offer customers free refreshments.

Leisure time

If you are feeling energetic, why not try the exciting new team game—baseball. Recently introduced from New York, the object of the game is to score more runs than the opposing team. Four bases are marked in a diamond shape on open ground and the two 9-player teams take turns batting and fielding. A run is made when a batter completes a circuit of all four bases.

Traveling musicians roam around the mining camps, playing popular songs on banjos.

Look out for the bell-ringers employed to draw crowds into the theaters.

 There are special mining songs such as "On the Banks of the Sacramento."

 Theater performers often tour the mining camps and towns.

Sightseers' tip San Francisco theaters such as the Metropolitan attract full houses most evenings. The cheaper seats are in the pit and the rear balconies.

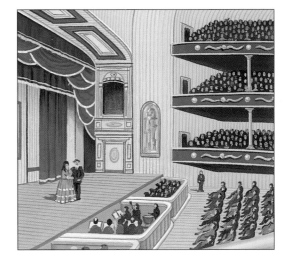

Baseball games are often played on the Sandlot—a park on the site of San Francisco's old cemetery.

Why not visit one of the many theaters that have sprung up in San Francisco over the last five years? Comedy and singing acts are very popular with audiences, but the latest rage is for child performers. Because of the shortage of women in California, actresses are always well received. Male actors, however, are often booed.

Redheaded Lotta Crabtree is the most famous child star. She sings, dances, recites poems, and does imitations of famous people.

21

Sutter's Mill

Captain John Sutter is a German immigrant. He moved to California in 1839 and acquired a large plot of land from the Mexican governor.

Make sure you visit Sutter's Mill, site of the first gold discovery. In 1847, Captain John Sutter needed lumber for his various building projects, and went into partnership with James Marshall, a carpenter, to build a mill. On January 24, 1848, Marshall was making his daily inspection of the sawmill when he discovered pieces of gold in the water.

Sightseers' tip Another historic building worth a visit is Mission Dolores. Founded by Franciscan monks in 1776, the tile-covered, white-walled church is dedicated to St. Francis. Take time to admire the gilded altar, painted ceilings, and Spanish manuscripts.

Sutter tried to keep quiet about the gold find on his land, but newspaper man Sam Brannan made sure news of the gold spread far and wide. He was drumming up trade for his new store, which he had amply stocked with picks, shovels, and pans.

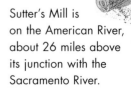

Sutter's Mill is on the American River, about 26 miles above its junction with the Sacramento River.

Sutter is not profiting from the gold rush as much of his land has been taken by miners.

 Mission Dolores is a Roman Catholic church founded by Spanish monks.

 Look out for paintings by Native Americans on the ceilings of Mission Dolores.

It was not until the discovery of gold in California was confirmed by President James Polk in December 1848 that the gold rush truly began. In 1849, nearly 100,000 prospectors passed through San Francisco on their way to the gold mines.

Sutter's Fort makes a good stopover for travelers. It has a blacksmith's shop and a grain mill, and you can camp there overnight. The fort is near Sacramento, the capital of California.

23

The wild west

The state of California is famed for its breathtaking and varied scenery. In the north, rugged, snowcapped mountain ranges and dense fir, pine, and redwood forests dominate the landscape. In contrast, southern California boasts beautiful beaches, the scorching Mojave Desert, and Death Valley, the hottest place in the United States.

Native Americans call Death Valley "Tomesha"—the land where the ground is on fire. This is because it gets so hot that the valley floor shimmers.

California is home to many strange and unique plants. The recently named Joshua trees in southern California can grow as tall as 30 feet. Some are believed to be over 1,000 years old.

California is a vast state with few roads. Travel can often be slow and treacherous.

The San Andreas Fault runs through the state, so earthquakes are always possible.

Look out for the many different Native American tribes in California.

Vaqueros (Californio cowboys) keep cattle from wandering off ranch land.

While traveling around California you may come across a Californio cattle ranch. Californios are descendants of the original Spanish settlers. Since the beginning of the gold rush, many Californios have abandoned their ranches to seek their fortunes in the mines.

Sightseers' tip

The largest trees in the world are found in northern California. The redwoods, or sequoias, can grow to heights of over 300 feet and live for over 3,000 years. Remember to look out for the wildlife—deer, foxes, and black bears all live in this area.

25

Native American tribes

If you need a break from the hustle and bustle of San Francisco, why not visit a Native American village? The 50 different tribes in California are hunter-gatherers and are very peaceful. They may, however, be suspicious of strangers—the gold rush is destroying their traditional way of life.

Sightseers' tip The Miwok tribe lives in round bark houses called *u-ma-cha*, and in the middle of the village is a large ceremonial house. The Miwoks wear feather costumes during their ceremonial dances.

Native Americans have few rights. Legally, they can be treated as slaves.

Acorns are a staple food—they are crushed and made into a gruel.

Native American crafts would be a good souvenir of your trip.

Many Californian tribes are famed for their detailed basketry.

Strings of dentalium shells are highly valued and are often used as money by Native American tribes in California. The longer the shell, the greater the value.

The constant activity in and around rivers by gold miners has polluted the water and killed many fish. It has also weakened oak trees, affecting the acorn harvest on which Native Americans depend. Many tribes have also been wiped out by diseases brought into the area by the miners, or suffered terrible persecution at the hands of the prospectors. It seems unlikely that Native American traditions will survive much longer.

Native Americans make very comfortable leather shoes called moccasins. Sometimes they will trade these for miners' boots.

27

Survival guide

Visitors to California should remember that it is still in the process of becoming a state. Things are not well organized yet—laws are invented off the cuff, transportation is limited, and life is very rough and ready. Prices are very high because most goods have to be shipped to San Francisco.

Law and order

To counter the lack of law enforcement, a group of San Francisco citizens banded together in 1851 and formed a "Vigilance Committee." Criminal offenders are hauled before the Committee and made to account for their actions. Very often the accused is flogged as punishment, but for serious crimes, such as murder, the punishment is hanging. The Committee makes its own rules and is known to punish people without trial.

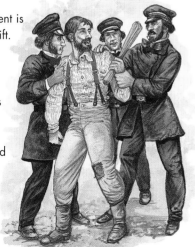

Punishment is often swift. It is not unheard of for criminals to be caught, tried, and hanged on the same day.

Health

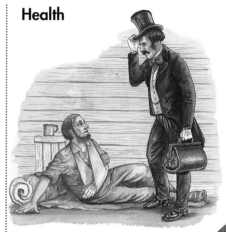

Try to avoid getting sick during your visit to California. Doctors will charge 30 grams of gold just for looking at your tongue!

Cholera, diphtheria, dysentery, and scurvy are all common diseases. Standing in cold water for long hours while panning for gold has given many miners rheumatism. Native American tribes have been badly affected by diseases carried by miners.

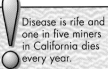
Disease is rife and one in five miners in California dies every year.

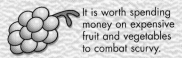
It is worth spending money on expensive fruit and vegetables to combat scurvy.

The Democratic Party is in power in most parts of California.

Administration

Fires are very common in San Francisco. The wooden buildings are very close together and can easily catch fire. Volunteer fire companies have formed all over the city to combat the frequent infernos. Membership in the fire companies is a great honor and there is much rivalry between the city's different companies.

After every fire, San Francisco is swiftly rebuilt. New buildings are often put up while fires are still smoldering.

Hundreds of men using long ropes haul the hose wagons and fire engines to the scene of the fire.

❓ Souvenir quiz

Take your time exploring California. It is a fascinating and varied land with plenty to see and do. Before you leave, test your knowledge with this fun quiz. You will find the answers on page 32.

1. Why are gold prospectors in California often called "forty-niners"?

a) Because California is the 49th state of the United States.

b) Because 1849 was the year that most prospectors traveled to California.

c) Because the average age of the prospectors is 49.

2. Shopping is expensive because most goods have to be shipped to San Francisco. Why are vegetables and dairy products so expensive?

a) Because agriculture has largely been abandoned as farm workers flock to the gold mines.

b) Because the land in California is very poor.

c) Because there is not much demand for fresh food.

3. Why is it sensible to bring a pair of sturdy boots with you to California?

a) Because they are considered the height of fashion.

b) To protect your feet from the mud that floods the streets of San Francisco.

c) To stop grizzly bears from picking up your scent.

4. How can you tell gold from fool's gold?

a) Fool's gold flakes when you bite it or hammer it.

b) Real gold is a different color from fool's gold.

c) Fool's gold has a distinct odor, while real gold is odorless.

5. Miners in California have coined many new words and expressions. What is "firewater"?

a) A unique natural phenomenon in Death Valley where flames rise from a pool of water.

b) A lake near San Francisco from which water is pumped to fight the city's many fires.

c) A nickname used by miners to describe alcoholic drinks.

6. The largest trees in the world can be found in California. What are they?

a) Joshua trees.

b) Redwood trees.

c) Oak trees.

7. Baseball is a new team game that is becoming very popular in California. What is a run?

a) A circuit of the four bases.

b) The name of the field.

c) A bet on the outcome of a game.

8. Gold was discovered at the site of Sutter's Mill in 1848. Who actually made the discovery?

a) Captain John Sutter, owner of the mill.

b) Sam Brannan, a newspaper owner.

c) James Marshall, a carpenter.

9. Native American tribes have had their traditional way of life destroyed by the gold rush. What do many Californian tribes use as money?

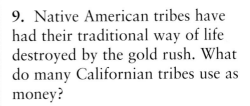

a) They don't use money—all goods are bartered (exchanged).

b) Gold and gems.

c) Strings of dentalium shells.

10. What is the usual punishment for murder?

a) Flogging.

b) Life imprisonment.

c) Death by hanging.

Index

Acknowledgments

Kingfisher would like to thank
Noreen Studdart for additional research.

The consultant
Christina Parker, B.A., P.G.C.E. is Education Officer at the American Museum in Britain, Bath, England.

Picture Research Manager
Jane Lambert

Inklink Firenze illustrators
Simone Boni, Alessandro Rabatti, Lorenzo Pieri, Luigi Critone, Lucia Mattioli, Francisco Petracchi, Theo Caneschi.

Additional illustrations
Peter Dennis, Shirley Tourret.

Picture credits
b = bottom, c = center, l = left, r = right, t = top
p.5tl Science Museum/ET Archive; p.6tl Peter Newark's American Pictures; p.10cl The Anthony Blake Photo Library; p.11cr Christie's Images; p.12tr The Bancroft Library/University of California, br Fitzwilliam Museum, University of Cambridge/The Bridgeman Art Library, London; p.14tl from *The Pocket Guide to California* by J.E. Sherwood, New York 1849, (RB1152)/The Huntington Library, San Marino, California, br Iris & B. Gerald Cantor Center for the Visual Arts at Stanford University; Stanford Family Collections, 12083; p.21br Brown Brothers; p.22tl Peter Newark's Pictures; p.23br Peter Newark's Pictures; p.24cl Corbis UK/David Paterson; p.29tr The Oakland Museum of California, Kahn Collection.

Every effort has been made to trace the copyright holders of the photographs. The publishers apologize for any inconvenience caused.

Souvenir quiz answers

1 = b) 2 = a) 3 = b) 4 = a) 5 = c) 6 = b) 7 = a) 8 = c) 9 = c) 10 = c)

This Sightseers guide is set in 1849–51.